FX!

LIGHTING
and SOUND

Jeff Larson and
Paul J. Larson M.Ed.

Consultants

Timothy Rasinski, Ph.D.
Kent State University

Lori Oczkus, M.A.
Literacy Consultant

Publishing Credits

Rachelle Cracchiolo, M.S.Ed., *Publisher*
Conni Medina, M.A.Ed., *Managing Editor*
Dona Herweck Rice, *Series Developer*
Emily R. Smith, M.A.Ed., *Content Director*
Stephanie Bernard/Susan Daddis, M.A.Ed., *Editors*
Robin Erickson, *Senior Graphic Designer*

The TIME logo is a registered trademark of TIME Inc. Used under license.

Image Credits: p.4 DeAgostini/Getty Images; p.5 Carlos Mora/Alamy Stock Photo; p.14 Pictorial Press Ltd/Alamy Stock Photo; p.15 (top) Pictorial Press Ltd/Alamy Stock Photo, (middle) Didreklama/Dreamstime.com; p.16 Lebrecht Music and Arts Photo Library/Alamy Stock Photo; p.17 PAINTING/Alamy Stock Photo; p.18 Wellcome Library/Internet Archive; p.19 (top) Theresa Knott used under Creative Commons BY-SA 2.5, (bottom) Royal College of Physicians in Edinburgh/Internet Archive; p.21 (top) Hulton Archive/Getty Images, (bottom) SSPL/Getty Images; p.22 SSPL/Getty Images; pp.26, 27 Glasshouse Images/Alamy Stock Photo; p.31 915 collection/Alamy Stock Photo; p.36 RKO Radio Pictures/Mercury Productions/AF archive/Alamy Stock Photo; p.40 Photos 12/Alamy Stock Photo; p.43 Underwood Archives/Getty Images; p.45 Universal Images Group North America LLC/Alamy Stock Photo; p.48 Randy Duchaine/Alamy Stock Photo; p.50 (top) Walt Disney Productions/Lisberger/Kushner/Ronald Grant Archive/Alamy Stock Photo, (bottom) Tristar Pictures/AF archive/Alamy Stock Photo; p.51 (top) Walt Disney Pictures/Photos 12/Alamy Stock Photo, (middle) Universal Pictures/Amblin Entertainment/Pictorial Press Ltd/Alamy Stock Photo, (bottom) Walt Disney Pictures/Photos 12/Alamy Stock Photo; p.53 jean-Paul Lozouet/Le Pictorium/Alamy Stock Photo; p.54 Aaron Camenisch, University of Kentucky; all other images from iStock and/or Shutterstock.

Teacher Created Materials

5301 Oceanus Drive
Huntington Beach, CA 92649-1030
http://www.tcmpub.com

ISBN 978-1-4938-3612-3

© 2017 Teacher Created Materials, Inc.
Printed in China
Nordica.082019.CA21901097

Table of Contents

In the Beginning

"All the world's a stage, And all the men and women merely players."

—Shakespeare's As You Like It, *Act II Scene VII*

Imagine this: You have been sent back in time some 15,000 years ago to southwestern France. It is a summer evening, but cool air moves over your skin. Darkness surrounds you, except for the flickering light of a nearby fire, around which a dozen people are gathered.

A deep voice resonates through the cavern. You realize the speaker is telling a story—a story of the hunt that has been captured in earthy tones on a wall of the cave. You glance around and see dozens of paintings: deer, bison, horses, and more. You realize these stories tell the tale of the people of Lascaux.

Could a moment such as this have been the origin of theater today? With the echoing voice and fire-lit speaker, were the elements of sound and lighting introduced in the **ritualistic** telling of the story of humankind? As you read on, imagine yourself on such a journey—where light and sound **illuminate** and amplify the stories of our lives.

Music to My Ears

Today, we can see the art on the cave walls, but we can't hear the Stone Age music that went with the paintings. In many caves, flutes crafted from bone have been found.

In a Cavern

Lascaux is the location of a collection of caves in southwestern France famous for their Paleolithic (early Stone Age) cave paintings. The paintings were discovered by four teens when they followed their dog down a narrow entrance into a cavern.

Setting the Stage

Can you imagine how lighting and sound affected early theatrical productions? Step back in time, first to ancient Greece and Rome and then to Asia, where the modern idea of theater developed.

It's Greek to Me

The history of Greek theater is rooted in religion. It began with festivals that honored the god Dionysus. From these festivals sprang the desire to share even more stories, and around 600 BC, the Greeks began building *theatrons*—large outdoor **amphitheaters**. These semicircular structures were constructed of stone—nestled on the slopes of hills—and are renowned for their outstanding **acoustics**.

Skene to Scene

The first skene to appear on the Greek stage was a small wooden hut. The entire cast for those early plays was the chorus, and they recited or sang the lines written by the playwright in unison. The actors changed in the skene. Over time, the skene grew larger.

The Theater at Epidaurus

When you search for the most beautiful and well preserved of the ancient theaters, you can do no better than the Theater at Epidaurus. With a capacity of 13,000 spectators, its acoustics are so superb that if a person standing in the orchestra tears a sheet of paper, it can be heard throughout the entire seating area!

Eventually, a two-story stone building called a *skene*—origin of the word *scene*—was built at the rear of the circular orchestra pit and stage. The skene usually had three doors on the front as well as doors on each side. These doors were used for entrances and exits. The skene served as a changing room for actors as well as a **resonator** for projecting the actors' voices toward the audience. Eventually, it served as the scenic background for the play. A narrow stage area for actors was created and called the *proskenion*—origin of the word ***proscenium***. The proscenium now serves as the arch at the front of a modern stage.

skene

proskenion

orchestra

Plays were performed during daylight hours, with a few festival performances timed to end just at sunset. Can you imagine how spectacular it must have been to exit the theater with hundreds of torches lit under a blackened sky to guide the spectators home? Some Greek playwrights incorporated the time of day into their scripts, and their show times were set accordingly.

The early Greek chorus, with as many as 50 people, used speech, song, and movement to help tell the story. Even though the theaters had great acoustics, the Greeks used additional strategies for **amplifying** voices. When an actor took his place on the stage, he wore a mask to help define his character. The mask also served as a **resonance** chamber. It helped an actor's lone voice to be heard throughout the entire theater space.

These are the ruins of the amphitheater in Epidaurus, Greece.

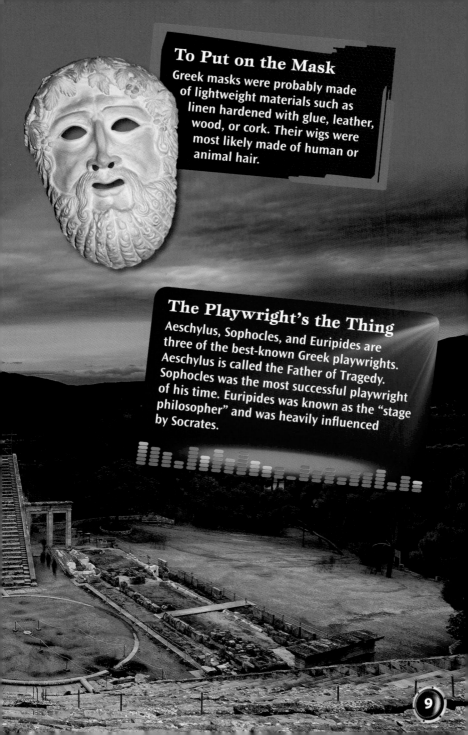

To Put on the Mask

Greek masks were probably made of lightweight materials such as linen hardened with glue, leather, wood, or cork. Their wigs were most likely made of human or animal hair.

The Playwright's the Thing

Aeschylus, Sophocles, and Euripides are three of the best-known Greek playwrights. Aeschylus is called the Father of Tragedy. Sophocles was the most successful playwright of his time. Euripides was known as the "stage philosopher" and was heavily influenced by Socrates.

Enter the Romans

The Romans took the Greeks' ingenious ideas and enhanced them. How did they do it?

The Romans further refined the theater. They extended the stage performance area over the orchestra, giving the rich and famous up-close-and-personal seats! They improved the theater's acoustics by enclosing the entire structure, not unlike the walls around the Colosseum in Rome. A *scaenae frons*, similar to the Greeks' skene, was located behind the stage. Usually two to three stories high, it provided a permanent backdrop for plays. It had three entrances on the ground floor and balconies on the others for cast members to use during performances. The *scaenae frons* was elaborately decorated using columns and statues.

The Romans continued using resonating masks for characters. The entire head of the actor was covered by a large and cumbersome mask. The substantial openings for the mouth and the eyes enhanced their exaggerated expressions. Now they were visible throughout the performance area. As for lighting, the Romans were presumably the first to use torches and oil lamps so that evening performances could occur.

Build It Up, Tear It Down

Many Roman theaters were temporary. Constructed of wood, they were torn down after the festivals for which they were built had concluded. This practice came from a law against permanent theater structures. The law lasted until AD 55.

It's Curtains for You!

By all accounts, the Romans were the first to use a curtain to open a play. It was dropped into a recessed area, or pit, once the play began. Theater curtains have evolved over time into many different styles.

On to Asia

The people of India were responsible for the earliest theater developments in the East, beginning in the first century AD. *The Natyashastra* is an Indian theater encyclopedia from those early years. It contains information on almost every part of theatrical art, including dance, music, stage design, and more.

Amphitheaters in Greece and Rome were large and located outdoors. In Asia, theaters were small and located indoors. Dramas were based on a style called *abhinaya*. They focused on exaggerated facial expressions and eye movements. These productions had to be seen close-up.

Greek plays started as tragedies, which told the story of a person's fate. A moral was always found at the heart of the story. Indian dramas, on the other hand, were based on the concept of **karma**. According to karma, a person is not thrown to the fates but can impact his own destiny, according to his actions.

Highly stylized forms of theater were the norm in China and Japan. Many productions were performed indoors with oil lamps, and magnificent costumes were key to each performance. Stories were told, but the emphasis was on performance rather than words. Traditions were incredibly important. Performances were extravagant, and acting styles were passed down through generations.

Noh Kidding!

Noh is the oldest major theater art still regularly performed today. Some Noh masks reflect stage lighting to show different emotions. An actor tilts the mask upward to reveal "brightening" and downward to reveal "clouding."

Shadow Puppetry

During the Ming dynasty, there were 40 to 50 shadow show troupes in the city of Beijing alone. Later, shadow puppetry was introduced to other Southeastern Asian countries, where it still remains popular.

Moving Indoors

From the **Passion plays** of the Middle Ages to **commedia dell'arte** of the Italian Renaissance, European theater evolved. But very little changed in light and sound. Even in the **Elizabethan Era**, plays were open to the **elements** and lit by the sun. Musicians sat in a balcony and played music. Sound effects were often created beneath the stage with musical instruments, sheets of metal, and even cannonballs.

As theater moved indoors, lighting became an issue. Designers found ways not only to light the stage but also to use lighting for effect. Here are some of the key players and inventions for stage lighting.

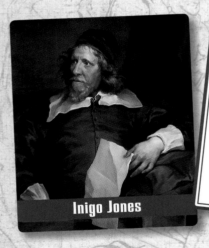

Inigo Jones

Inigo Jones (1573–1652) worked in one of the first indoor theaters in London. His most important innovation was adding reflectors to **footlight** candles. This directed more light onto the stage.

Magic Lantern

By the seventeenth century, many people were experimenting with using lanterns that had lenses to project images. In 1685, Johann Zahn showed how to project moving images using mechanical slides. This invention became known as a magic lantern.

Joseph Furttenbach

Joseph Furttenbach (1591–1667) moved chandeliers farther onto the stage to better light the actors. These were either border lights (overhead but hidden by curtains called borders) or wing lights (on the sides of the stage, hidden by curtains called wings or legs).

Chandelier

The first indoor theaters of London featured chandeliers. These long decorative fixtures contained dozens of candles. They lit the audience area (or *house*) as well as the stage.

Snuff Boy

Candlewicks onstage often had to be trimmed during a performance. This was the duty of the snuff boy. The change from daylight to darkness was created by the skill of these candle snuffers.

Drury Lane Theatre

David Garrick, the director of London's Drury Lane Theatre from 1747–1776, was one of the first to remove chandeliers and use lights on the stage to illuminate performers. The lights included wing lights and improved footlights called *floats*.

Oil Lamps

Oil lamps were widely used for lighting in the theater, especially as footlights. The wick, when placed in low-quality oil, gave off smoke and a foul smell. To solve for this, some theaters used high-quality olive oil. It offered more light with less smoke and a more pleasant odor.

Phillippe Jacques de Loutherbourg became a noted designer at London's Drury Lane Theater in 1773. He began using colored slides with concentrated lantern light. In this way, he created light changes for special effects such as moonlight, fire, and dawn.

Phillippe Jacques de Loutherbourg

Argand Burner

The Argand burner was invented in 1782. It was the first fundamental change in lamps for thousands of years. The burner created an airflow to support the burning oil and, later, gas. The Argand was 10 times brighter than a traditional oil lamp and required less maintenance.

THINK LINK

Through the eighteenth century, most lighting sources provided only general illumination. This means that the light was spread over a wide area. Today, theaters use general lighting and also a great deal of specific lighting.

- ◎ In what way might theater light be focused?
- ◎ What everyday object do you use that has a focused beam of light? How is this focused beam created?
- ◎ How do you think specific lighting improved the audiences' experiences?

New Inventions Light It Up!

New inventions dramatically changed theater lighting through the nineteenth century.

Gaslight

Argand burners, which used coal oil, gave way to **gaslights** in the nineteenth century. The gas came through a central distribution point called a *gas table*. The gas table regulated gas supply, which meant that brightness could be controlled. These tables became the first stage switchboards. Now, *any* lights connected to the gas pipe could be brightened or dimmed with the twist of a valve! In 1816, the Chestnut Street Theater in Philadelphia became the first gaslit theater in the world.

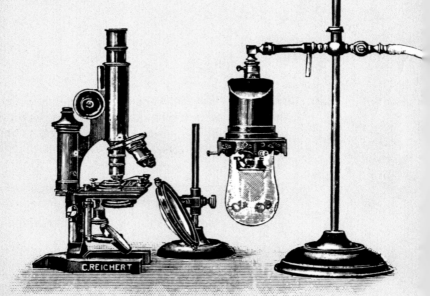

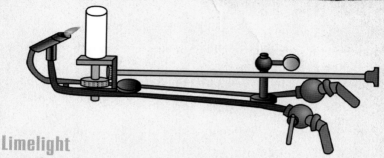

Limelight

The use of a strong, focused light arrived in 1816 when limelight was invented. Limelight used oxygen mixed with hydrogen to heat a block of limestone. It produced an intense and very white light, which used a reflector to shape the light into a narrow beam. Later, a lens was added to concentrate the beam even more. Today, a person "in the limelight" is the center of attention.

Arc Light

Later in the century, carbon arcs used reflectors and lenses to condense the light beams and produce extremely bright lights. The arc light could be used as both a spotlight and a floodlight. A sliding shutter between the source and the lens was used to dim the light. Huge electric batteries supplied electricity. But there were drawbacks. These lights were noisy, the lights flickered, and, as with the limelight, each needed the constant attention of a dedicated operator.

Shocking News

Phonograph Makes Magic with Sound
December 22, 1877

Mr. Edison and his new **phonograph** visited the offices of *Scientific American* in New York City. One staff member reports, "Mr. Thomas A. Edison recently came into this office, placed a little machine on our desk, and turned a crank. The machine inquired as to our health, asked how we liked the phonograph, informed us that it was very well, and bid us a cordial good night." Interest in the phonograph is high in the theater world.

For the manufacturing and sales rights to his device, Edison is to receive $10,000. He will also receive 20 percent of the profits. The machine is sure to be an instant success. Experts warn, though, that it is difficult to operate without training.

phonograph

Electric Light Sparks Excitement!

October 21, 1879

Thomas Edison

Edison is now developing an electric light company. He plans to build a system of power stations. The company will deliver the electricity needed to run his bulbs. Theatrical light designers are anxious to see what the lightbulb can bring to their lighting designs.

Thomas Edison created a workable electric light at his lab in Menlo Park, New Jersey. Mr. Edison regards this as his crowning triumph. He sees it as a model of simplicity and economy. Edison's goal was to devise a lamp that lasted longer and required less power than previous designs. Early models were not practical for daily use.

filament lamp

bulb

Savoy Installs First Electric Lighting System
October 10, 1881

Sir Joseph Swan's dream has come true! The Savoy Theater has gone electric. The stage is lit by 824 sixteen-candlepower Swan lamps. An additional 334 lights illuminate the seating area. The inventor of the **incandescent** lamp is thrilled!

The Savoy is a state-of-the-art theater. It is the first public building in the world to be lit entirely by electricity. Swan supplied some 1,200 Swan electric lamps. They are powered by a 120-horsepower generator located near the theater.

Richard D'Oyly Carte, owner of the Savoy, explained why he introduced electric light. "The greatest drawbacks to the enjoyment of the theatrical performances are, undoubtedly, the foul air and heat which pervade all theaters. As everyone knows, each gas burner consumes as much oxygen as many people and causes great heat beside. The incandescent lamps consume no oxygen and cause no perceptible heat." People in London are thrilled!

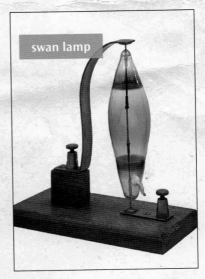

swan lamp

Smashing Success
December 28, 1881

Electric lighting has successfully been used throughout the Savoy Theater, not just in the house. At a recent performance, Savoy owner Mr. Carte stepped onstage and broke a glowing lightbulb. He hoped to demonstrate for the shocked audience the safety of the bulb. The bulb did not explode or exude dangerous or foul odors. The audience cheered its response.

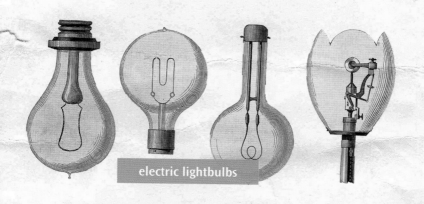

electric lightbulbs

Melodrama

In Victorian Era London, the Savoy featured comic operas and romantic dramas known as **melodramas**. Each performance featured music ("melo") played along with the story ("drama"). The music **underscored** exaggerated emotions and stylized characters, like those seen in early forms of Asian theater. This acting style lived on in many silent movies, and the format is a precursor to today's musicals.

How Does the Phonograph Work?

The phonograph is a triumph of engineering! The movement of the cylinder and groove needs to be precisely aligned in order for the machine to work. This is a difficult thing to do and requires superb engineering.

1. A large horn is connected to the phonograph to collect nearby sound. These waves of sound then travel down the horn and vibrate a flexible **diaphragm**.

2. The diaphragm is attached to a **stylus**. The stylus pushes down into a cylinder covered in wax or tinfoil.

3. Turning the handle causes the cylinder to spin. The stylus moves up and down, turning sound vibrations into indentations or grooves in the wax or tinfoil.

4. Sound is reproduced by moving the stylus back along the indentations. Since these grooves correspond to specific vibrations, the original sounds recorded are played back through the horn.

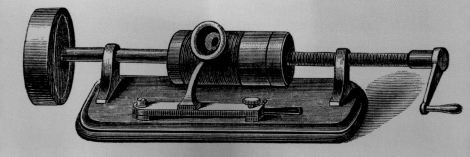

THE EDISON CONCERT PHONOGRAPH

TRADE
Thomas A. Edison
MARK

Copy That!

In the early days of the phonograph, there was no way to mass-produce copies of a recorded performance. A few copies were created by huddling multiple phonographs near the performers. Each phonograph produced one copy of the performance.

Here Comes the Cinema

As we have seen, the origins of "moving pictures" date back as far as the seventeenth century and the magic lantern. But in the late nineteenth century, Edison and others began using strips of **celluloid** film to really get things moving.

Film Revolution

The first films in the 1890s were simple single shots of daily life. These films were viewed by one person at a time on Edison's **kinetoscope**. **Nickelodeons** were storefronts redesigned to show these early motion pictures.

In 1894, the Lumière brothers of France were given a piece of kinetoscope film, and they studied it. By the next year, the brothers had invented their own device. It combined a camera with a printer and a projector. They called it the *cinématographe*. It was much smaller and lighter than the kinetoscope and had to be cranked by hand. Their new invention was a closely guarded secret until the first public screening on December 28, 1895. The invention was an instant hit!

The brothers began to open theaters, called cinemas, to show their films. By April 1896, they had opened cinemas in London, Brussels, and New York.

Black Maria

Edison's film studio, nicknamed Black Maria, opened the roof to let in natural light. The whole structure was on a giant turntable that rotated to follow the sun!

man looking in a kinetoscope

Méliès Movie Maker

Georges Méliès was a French pioneer in motion pictures and the first to film fictional stories. Méliès made more than 400 films and developed techniques such as stop-motion, the cross-dissolve, double exposure, and frame painting—the first cinema special effects!

Lights, Camera, Action!

Moving pictures quickly became a cultural phenomenon. At first, filmmakers, much like the early dramatists, used natural light in making their movies. Then, directors of the early silent films started to explore the use of artificial light.

In 1901, Peter Cooper Hewitt invented the mercury-vapor lamp, which made it practical to shoot films indoors. And remember those carbon-arc spotlights? They were adapted from the theater to film, while **diffusion screens** were adapted from still photography. The spotlights allowed for bright lights on a dark set, and the screens provided soft lights for close-ups.

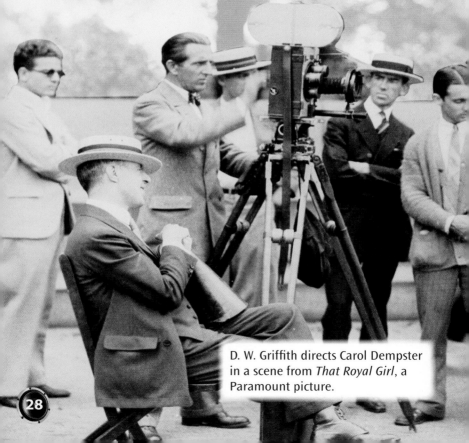

D. W. Griffith directs Carol Dempster in a scene from *That Royal Girl*, a Paramount picture.

D. W. Griffith was the first great director of the Silent Era. He and his cameraman, Billy Bitzer, began shooting faces close-up. Griffith created soft lighting effects by "bouncing" **backlight** to redirect it onto actors' faces. He also used high-contrast lighting to cast shadows across actors and sets. Another new technique was cross-cutting. This involved inter-cutting action from different scenes to help build tension.

Cecil B. DeMille was another innovative director. He pioneered indoor lighting. Before DeMille, indoor night scenes were tinted blue to show night. Meanwhile, the sun blazed through windows and doors! DeMille shot night scenes with both artificial lights and practical, or source, lights. These lights, such as desk lamps, appear as a part of the scene. His distinctive style soon became the norm for films.

Larger Than Life

Orson Welles was a dynamo who changed the way stories were told on stage, on the radio, and in film. His innovative style shaped the future of each medium.

June 16, 1937: The musical *The Cradle Will Rock*, directed by Orson Welles, is scheduled to open on Broadway with elaborate sets and a full orchestra.

But the U.S. government's Works Progress Administration (WPA) shuts down the show because of budget cuts.

Producer John Houseman leads the audience to a new venue!

At the Gate

When he was 16, Orson Welles traveled across Europe. In Ireland, he wrote this note to the manager of The Gate Theater: "Orson Welles, star of the New York Theater Guild, would consider appearing in one of your productions and hopes you will see him for an appointment." Welles's note led to his first professional theater role!

After shaking things up on Broadway, Welles set his sights on the nation. His radio broadcast of *War of the Worlds* changed the airways.

The Martians Are Invading!

About 15 minutes into *War of the Worlds*, every phone at CBS began ringing at once. All the callers were hysterical!

The headlines in the newspaper the following day tell a different story.

Birth of Radio

Radio originated in the nineteenth century as "wireless telegraph." By the 1920s, newly invented vacuum tubes enabled the first radio broadcasts. By 1938, radio provided a variety of programming, including musical performances, dramas, and comedies. Listeners also experienced the news in a whole new way.

Welles was soon courted by Hollywood. He began shooting his first feature-length film in July 1940. *Citizen Kane* is considered by many to be *the* greatest film ever made. Welles co-wrote, directed, produced, and even starred in the film!

Many critics argue that *Citizen Kane* is the first **film noir**. Film noir is a **genre** that uses a dark, moody atmosphere to enhance the mysterious events taking place. Cinematographer Gregg Toland created a dramatic world of light and shadow. Much of this was done by using a low intensity **key light**. This allowed the **fill light** and **backlight** to dominate.

The Battle Over Citizen Kane

Many people saw *Citizen Kane* as a bleak portrait of real-life wealthy newspaper owner, William Randolph Hearst. When Hearst learned about the film, he tried to shut it down. Hollywood executives tried to buy *Citizen Kane* so they could burn the negatives. Hearst's friends even tried to intimidate theaters into refusing to show the movie.

Citizen Kane made advances on many fronts. Its biggest innovation was the use of **deep focus**. Deep focus refers to having everything in the frame—even the background—in focus at the same time. This technique requires the cinematographer to combine bright lighting and a small **aperture** to produce the effect. The illusion of deep focus can be created with optical tricks or by **compositing** two images.

Citizen Kane introduced Hollywood to other techniques as well. One innovation is known as the wipe. One image is "wiped" off the screen by another. Welles also experimented with unusual camera angles.

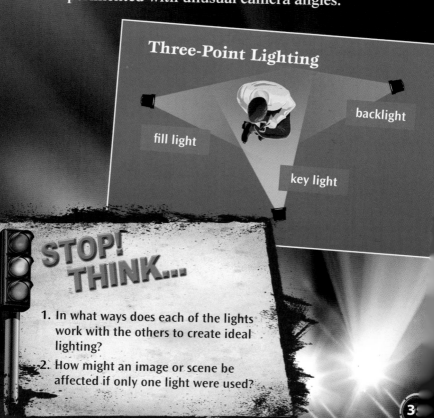

Three-Point Lighting

backlight

fill light

key light

STOP! THINK...

1. In what ways does each of the lights work with the others to create ideal lighting?

2. How might an image or scene be affected if only one light were used?

Designers Transform the Stage

As theater and cinema evolved, so did light design. Designers weren't just lighting the actors on the stage. They were contributing to the way that stories were told.

Revolutionary Designers

In the late 1800s, Adolphe Appia developed new theories about stage lighting. He believed that light did more than illuminate actors and scenery. Appia thought light was the primary element of theater. It fused together all aspects of a production and reflected the changing mood of the work.

Lighting Console

Frederick Bentham developed the lighting **console** in 1936. A lighting console, or light board, is used to control the intensity of the lights. Lights were also controlled remotely, allowing the operator to see what was being lit. Early consoles looked just like organs, so the operator "played" the lights!

David Belasco liked naturalism in acting and in design. This impulse pushed him to innovate lighting. In 1904, Belasco and his electrician, Louis Hartman, developed and refined new instruments. The two also set a standard of realism in stage lighting that anticipated the realism of motion pictures.

Visionary Norman Bel Geddes also started his career in the theater in the early twentieth century. Once, he was outfitting a theater with incandescent spotlights. He moved the border lights from over the stage to over the front of the audience, pointing at the stage. Bel Geddes noticed that the lights picked up facial features and lit actors' eyes in ways that border and footlights could not. Their concentrated beams also lit the actors without spilling onto the scenery.

Cyclorama

In 1902, Mariano Fortuny developed an elaborate system of soft reflected light. He bounced arc lights off a dome-shaped wall, lighting up stretched silk fabric. The produced light, called a *cyclorama* or *cyc*, was quite similar to natural lighting. A cyc gives the illusion of infinite space. This is a great way to create a spectacular sky and other background effects.

Workers in Light: First Dedicated Designers

Take a minute to meet a few designers who shed some light on modern design.

Abe Feder

» I invented the position of lighting designer.

» I designed the lighting for over 300 Broadway shows.

» I wrote the unit on stage lighting in the classic text *Producing the Play*, 1940.

Jean Rosenthal

» I am known for creating pools of light onstage. My work made light of equal importance to other design in shaping the work.

» My most important work was with the Martha Graham Dance Company, the New York City Ballet, and some of the big musicals of the 1950s and '60s.

» My friend Thomas Skelton said, "Jeannie Rosenthal invented dance lighting."

Peggy Clark

» I created my first stage show when I was only five. I built a marionette theater from a cardboard box, a ball of string, and my collection of dolls.

» In 1938, I began assisting several prominent scene designers on Broadway.

» I went on to design lighting for some of the biggest hits on Broadway.

Thomas Skelton

» I designed lighting for dance. I generally worked with the Joffrey Ballet.

» I designed lighting for 63 Broadway shows.

» I was a master at identifying and using the five qualities of light. These qualities are intensity, form, color, direction, and movement. They are the lighting designer's tools.

Gels and Color Mixing

Lighting gels were introduced in the late 1800s. These thin colored sheets were placed in front of a light to change the light color onstage. By the 1900s, designers had begun mixing different colors from different lights to create more lighting effects with fewer instruments.

RGB

When red, green, and blue paint are mixed, a grayish-brown color appears. What happens when red, green, and blue lights are shined on an object? They make white! This is called additive color mixing.

Television Takes Over

It's amazing to think that television was first successfully demonstrated as early as 1928. Philo Farnsworth created it. To transmit moving images, each image must be broken up into pinpoints of light. These points are sent as electrical impulses. The impulses are collected at the receiving end. There, they are translated back into light. The result is a reproduction of the original image!

Before Farnsworth's breakthrough, television systems were mechanical rather than electronic. They used large revolving discs. One disc sat at the transmitting end and another at the receiving end. The discs were used to break up the image. They had to revolve at the same instant and speed or the image would blur.

At first, television sets were mostly novelties. The 1950s and 1960s saw the Golden Era of television. In 1947, fewer than 40,000 sets were in use across the country. By 1960, that number had grown to nearly 60 million.

Another revolution came in 1956 with the use of videotape. The tape allowed for the recording of live events that could be broadcast later. Then in 1964, color came into use.

Funny Face

Early television cameras had their limitations. Cameras used blue sensitive film, which created problems with lighting and color tones. Red and yellows looked black, while lighter blues appeared an eerie white. To resolve this problem, actors wore black lipstick and green makeup, which created more natural tones in the grayscale onscreen.

STOP! THINK...

Use the background image to answer the questions.

- ◉ Compare and contrast the television on the page to a modern one.
- ◉ How do you think the vertical and horizontal sync knobs helped television viewers?

VHF

UHF

Brightness

Contrast

Vertical Sync

Horizontal Sync

Volume

Power

Off   On

How Does It Work?

How does a TV camera capture and transmit an image to your screen? The camera translates light from an image into an electrical current, piece by piece. These "pieces" are dots arranged in tiny lines that together form an image. When this current reaches a television, the lines are put back together. Each line is "painted" across the TV as the current of electrons hits specific dots on the inside of the screen. The current recreates the lines from the camera on the TV screen. The painting happens so fast that your eyes recognize the lines as one picture! If you've ever seen an older television, you've noticed that the thick, chunky screens have been replaced by thinner flat-screen TVs. Newer TVs still "paint" images across their screens but do so electronically rather than by using a signal. These new TVs can also paint more lines faster, meaning that images appear clearer and more realistic.

Sound and Light

There are waves of energy and light moving around us all the time. Television and radio transmissions, gamma radiation from space, and heat in the atmosphere are always present. Scientists refers to all of these as **electromagnetic** radiation. They are electromagnetic because they have both electric and magnetic characteristics. Physicists identify them according to the frequency of their wavelengths, going from high to low. A wave with a lot of energy might be a gamma ray or an x-ray. A wave with a low frequency has less energy and could be a television or radio wave.

Television Evolution

For over 60 years, TVs used cathode ray tubes to display images. In recent years, this technology has been replaced with thinner liquid crystal display (LCD) and plasma screens.

The Recorded Sound Revolution

Interestingly, silent films were not as silent as you might imagine. As in the theater, live musical accompaniment was an important part of the experience, whether through a simple organ or a one-hundred-piece orchestra.

All of that began to change in 1927 with *The Jazz Singer*. It was the first feature film to use synced sound sequences. In these new films, called "talkies," sound effects were made to sync with the action.

Synced sound presented many challenges for sound recordists, who were initially scarce. Hollywood had to call on the talents of professionals from theater and radio. Sound effects had been used in the theater for centuries and extensively in live broadcasts of radio dramas.

The sound revolution affected the types of lights filmmakers used. Incandescent lights, called "inkies," replaced carbon arcs in the mid 1920s. They were a better match for the new film stock in use. Also, inkies are silent, which was important when films moved into the sound era.

Frame Rate

At first, there was no fixed speed in which films were shot or projected. This speed is called the **frame rate**, and it tended to vary from 16 to 20 frames per second (fps). By the late 1920s, because of sync sound, the U.S. film standard was set at 24 fps. Lower frame rates in silent films are the reason for their sometimes choppy movements.

The art of creating sounds for film is called Foley. Jack Foley created sound for the film *Show Boat*. The film was projected onto a screen while Foley and his crew recorded a single track of audio to capture live sound effects. The timing had to be perfect so that footsteps and closing doors synchronized with the actors' motions.

Foley Sound

Care to try some Foley sound effects? For beating horse hooves, strike coconut half-shells or small plastic bowls on a tabletop. For a crackling fire, crinkle **cellophane**.

Good Vibrations

As the twentieth century progressed, technology advanced rapidly. Like waves, these changes were rippling through the world of sound. Foley artists gave way to skilled sound operators, and microphones went wireless.

What's That Sound?

In the 1950s, magnetic recording tape arrived as a way to record and play back sound. Magnetic tape was a huge leap forward. Playback began with the push of a button, meaning that the timing of sound **cues** was much more accurate. The tape could also be spliced, or cut, just like film. That meant it could be edited, with sounds arranged and rearranged depending on the needs of the show.

The 1950s also saw the introduction of the playback mixing console. It was called a **mixer** or a mixing desk. The tape playback machine (or deck) and mixer could be housed in a booth at the back of the theater. Now, just one operator could run all the sound cues from the sound booth during a theater production!

The film industry also began using magnetic tape at this time. Directors could make movies with better sound quality. The previous method produced background noise. However, using magnetic tape was costly for sound production and could only be integrated at the end of filming.

On Track

Tape recording allowed recordings to be made in multiple parts, or tracks. These tracks were mixed and edited with very little loss in quality. Before magnetic tape, gramophone records were recorded in one take.

Wireless Technology

Wireless microphones arrived in the 1960s. They are called "body mics" because they are placed on the actors' bodies. The first body mics were large and expensive. Smaller and more affordable mics came about in the 1980s.

Body mics send their signals to the mixing desk via a small radio transmitter hidden somewhere on the actor. The mic itself is often placed in an actor's hair or taped to his or her cheek. The quality of sound is extremely high!

Broadway musicals took up the new technology. Now, a sound operator could balance the volume of an actor's voice with the music. The mixing desk was also moved into the seating area. The move helped the sound operator hear what the audience hears and adjust the sound accordingly.

Digital Sound

Popular music in the 1970s inspired a new wave of filmmakers. Directors such as Francis Ford Coppola and Martin Scorsese took a deeper look at how sound effects, dialogue, and music blended into movie soundtracks. They began to use digital resources to do this.

Meanwhile, in the theater, digital and computer-based media replaced **analog** media. Sound was freed from the mechanical editing, cutting, and rearranging processes. Digital recording also allowed for **sampling** and **looping**.

Sound Designer

In the film industry, the role of sound designer was defined by director Coppola and sound designer Walter Murch as "an individual ultimately responsible for all aspects of a film's audio track, from the dialogue and sound effects recording to the re-recording (mix) of the final track."

Sampling and Looping

Instead of cutting a piece of tape, a digital recording can be sampled by isolating a small section, or clip, of a song or effect and storing it. The sample can then be looped, or played repeatedly. So, for example, a 20-minute rainstorm could be looped from a one-minute sound file.

CGI

The arrival of the computer in the mid-twentieth century led the way for new digital technologies. One of the most significant was computer-generated imagery. Known as CGI, it allows filmmakers to create any image they can imagine on screen in a realistic way. Here are a few of the game changers in CGI history.

Terminator 2: Judgment Day

CGI makes a character appear to change form and shape. The 1992 film won the Academy Award® for Best Visual Effects.

Toy Story

Pixar Studios created the first fully CGI feature-length film. *Toy Story* led to a revolution in film animation.

Tron

Using CGI, filmmakers placed actors inside a realistic, three-dimensional video-game world.

Light and Shadow

CGI artists must accurately capture how people, animals, and objects reflect light. This digital lighting mimics how shadows and highlights appear in real life, making animated scenes appear more realistic.

Beauty and the Beast

Computers added depth to animation. Maybe that's why this was the first animated film to be nominated for the Academy Award® in the Best Picture category in 1992.

Jurassic Park

Moviemakers blended life-size puppets with CGI dinosaurs to create a jaw-dropping world. It's hard to believe that the dinosaurs are not real!

Interview with a Projection Designer

A projection designer is in charge of creating all still and movie images used in a stage production. The edited images are uploaded to be shown during a performance. In the following interview, Jeff Larson talks about his work as a projection designer.

Paul: *How did you become interested in projection design?*

Jeff: For me, projections bring together many avenues of interest. Filmmaking, photography, directing, and set design all come into play. The wonderful challenge of creating projections for the theater is that each production asks for a different set of solutions. For one project, I may work a lot with live cameras and even be onstage. For another, I may create animations to connect scenes. I may even work with historical photos to mimic the texture and energy of a place and time. That variety is exciting.

Paul: *How do projections relate to the other design elements?*

Jeff: Projections are closely related to both scenic and lighting design. For the projected images to be seen, the set has to feature surfaces that can receive the images. There might even be screens that can display them. Deciding what these surfaces are is a key part of the early design process. A balance must be found between the lighting and the projections so that both actors and images can be seen.

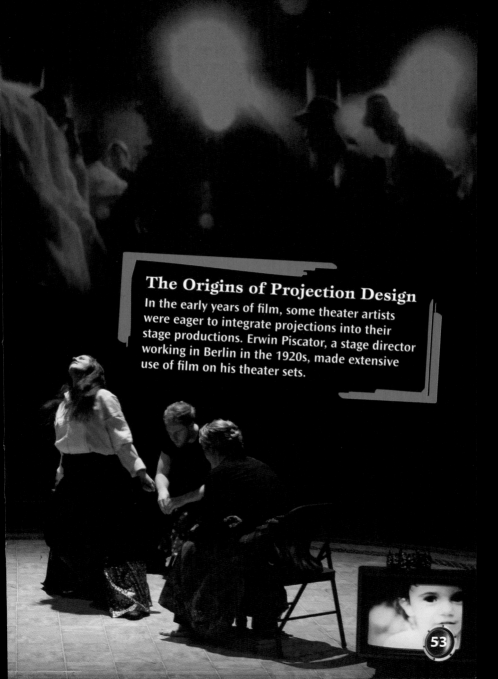

The Origins of Projection Design

In the early years of film, some theater artists were eager to integrate projections into their stage productions. Erwin Piscator, a stage director working in Berlin in the 1920s, made extensive use of film on his theater sets.

Paul: *What are the highlights and challenges of working with directors?*

Jeff: It depends on the director! One of the biggest challenges is to "see" the proposed design in the early stages of design and rehearsal. Sometimes, visual ideas can be difficult to describe. The challenge becomes finding creative ways to simulate, or mock up, the proposed design. One thing I personally love about working with a director is discovering imaginative ways to help tell the story.

Paul: *Do you have any advice for someone interested in learning more about projection design?*

Jeff: See great films and figure out what makes them great. Attend a theater performance and ask yourself how stories are told—then imagine how they can be told differently. Tinker—with a video camera, with computer software, with animation. Shoot a scene with your friends and figure out how to edit it. Explore.

Advance to the Rear

If you want to create a digital background that appears to be right behind an actor, you might try rear projection. It gives you a stark contrast.

Looking to the Future

The future of lighting and sound on stage and screen is dynamic. After the open flame and incandescent bulb, stage lighting was revolutionized. Now, **LED** lights produce millions of colors and are reshaping lighting design. Music and sound are changing, too, through digital media. What used to take days in a studio can be done quickly and almost anywhere. Projection technology, too, is part of the exciting future of design.

Computer software continues to evolve at a brisk pace. Every change allows the designer more artistic control over light and sound. And cues for all needs can be run through a single computer! The possibilities for design expand every day.

The changes we have seen through history have been amazing and a testament to human ingenuity. Each era seems to bear a catalyst that ignites an innovative flame. It sets off a flurry of creativity. And just as the sound of thunder rolls on after the lightning strikes, so will the innovations of entertainment light and sound.

A New Illuminator?

Today, we have the technology to create a million colors with one instrument! LEDs—or light-emitting diodes—save energy and operate without much heat. They can even be moved remotely with the touch of a button!

Glossary

acoustics—the qualities or characteristics of a space that determine the quality of sound in it.

amphitheaters—large structures in an open space with seats rising in semicircular rows where performances take place

amplifying—making a sound louder

analog—a device or process in which data is represented by physical quantities that change continuously

aperture— a small hole in a camera lens that regulates the amount of light that goes through it

backlight—light that illuminates the subject from the rear to provide definition and small highlights around the edge of the subject

cellophane—a clear, thin plastic material used for wrapping

celluloid—a hard, flammable plastic that was used to make film

commedia dell'arte—Italian form of theater that emphasized ensemble and improvisational work

compositing—combining two or more visual elements to make a single image

console—a piece of equipment that contains the controls for lighting or sound

cues—reminders (words, phrases, or stage business) to an actor/actress to begin specific actions

diaphragm—the membrane on a phonograph that vibrates, amplifying the sound before it passes through the horn

diffusion screens—clear screens that reduce light

electromagnetic—having to do with the magnetic field produced by an electric current

elements—weather conditions; especially violent or severe weather

Elizabethan Era—time in English history marked by the reign of Queen Elizabeth I

fill light—light on the opposite side of the key light that fills the shadows

film noir—a style of filmmaking noted for elements such as cynical heroes, stark lighting effects, frequent use of flashbacks, and intricate plots

footlight—a row of lights set at floor level at the front of a stage, used to provide a part of the general production lighting

frame rate—the number of frames in an animation that are displayed each second

gaslights—lights produced when gas burns

genre—a way to sort music, art, and/or literature, noting similarities in style, form, or theme

illuminate—to light up

incandescent—producing bright light along with great heat

karma—the energy created by a person's actions that some believe causes good or bad things to happen to that person

key light—light that is the brightest; placed to the side of the camera and subject so that one side is well lit and the other is in shadow

kinetoscope—an early instrument for watching a moving picture

LED—light emitting diode; a device that lights up when electricity passes through it

looping—repeating a section of sound media

melodramas—dramatic pieces with exaggerated characters and exciting events intended to appeal to the emotions

mixer—a device that controls the recording of sounds that go with a play, a film, or a television show

nickelodeons—early motion picture theaters where films could be seen, usually for the ticket price of a nickel

Passion plays—plays that detail the death of Jesus Christ

phonograph—a sound-reproducing machine using records in the form of cylinders or discs

proscenium—the arch that separates a stage from the auditorium

resonance—sound produced by an object vibrating due to a nearby source of sound

resonator—an object for increasing sound, such as a mask

ritualistic—doing something in a particular situation and in the same way each time

sampling—taking a small part of a song and using it as part of another song

stylus—the sharp metal piece on a phonograph that pushes into the wax to create (and play back) a recording

underscored—stressed

Index

Check It Out!

Books

Belli, Mary Lou and Dinah Lenney. 2006. *Acting for Young Actors: The Ultimate Teen Guide*. Back Stage Books.

McLemore, Anna-Marie. 2015. *The Weight of Feathers*. A Thomas Donne Book for St. Martin's Griffin.

Schumacher, Thomas and Jeff Kurtii. 2008. *How Does the Show Go On? An Introduction to the Theater*. Disney Editions.

Soto, Gary. 2006. *Novio Boy: A Play*. HMH Books for Young Readers.

Wood, Maryrose. 2008. *My Life: The Musical.* Delacorte Books for Young Readers.

Zadoff, Allen. 2011. *My Life, The Theater, and Other Tragedies*. Egmont USA.

Videos/DVD

How We Got to Now with Steven Johnson: The History and Power of Great Ideas. 2014. Public Broadcasting System.

Website

Academy of Motion Picture Arts and Sciences. *Science and Technology*. http://www.oscars.org/.

Try It!

You've been hired to create the light and sound effects for your favorite children's book or novel, which is being transformed into a film or play.

- What story will you choose? Make sure it hasn't already been made into a film!
- Choose an important scene from the book or novel.
- What sound effects will be needed? What materials will you use to produce them?
- What time of day does this scene take place?
- What kind of lighting will you need to ensure that the author's tone comes across?
- If you can, create the scene and film it!

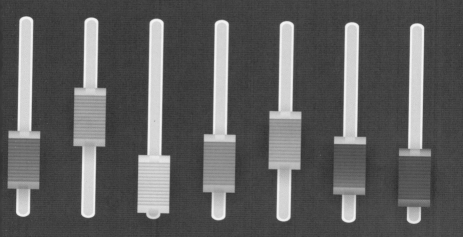

About the Authors

Paul Larson is a recently retired teacher and administrator with the Chino Valley Unified School District in California. A beloved and active member of his community, Paul and his wife, Karen, are also the founders of the Chino Community Theater and the Chino Community Children's Theater. The Larsons have three children and one granddaughter.

Jeff Larson is a designer, a curator, and an educator. He creates projection designs for Big Dance Theater. Jeff is co-curator of the Obie award-winning Brooklyn-based performance series, CATCH. He is an adjunct faculty member of the Department of Design for Stage and Film and the Experimental Theater Wing at New York University's Tisch School of the Arts.